Secrets of Financial Planning

Patrick Peterhans – CFP®

Disclaimer / Limits of Liability

Before I start the book, here is what my lawyers told me to add:

The author and publisher of this book and the accompanying materials have used his best effort in preparing this handbook. Use and/or reliance on this handbook are strictly at the purchaser's own risk. *Financial Solutions Box dot com* shall not be liable for incidental, indirect, special or consequential damages resulting from reading this book or for lost profits, savings or revenues of any kind.

Secrets of Financial Planning – 2nd Edition
Copyright 2008 by Focused Financial Planning, Inc.
ISBN: 978-0-6152-3541-7

Published by:
Focused Financial Planning, Inc.
dba FinancialSolutionsBox.com
1615 Pearl Street Ste B
Boulder, CO 80302
303-951-4034

To my family, my wife Nicole,
my daughters Nayana and Soklyn,
and my son Yannick.

Introduction

Congratulations and thank you for buying my "Secrets of Financial Planning" book. My goal with this book is to get you on the right path to a secure financial future, and to encourage you to take full responsibility for your financial well-being.

Let me introduce myself first. My name is Patrick Peterhans. I'm a Certified Financial Planner with my own practice in Boulder, Colorado. I've been helping my clients with their unique financial needs for over ten years. My clients are as diverse as the subject of Financial Planning itself, which makes my work very exciting.

This book will provide you with a short, but thorough introduction into the vast world of Financial Planning. It will touch on all the important aspects to guide you on the path to a safe and secure financial future. Throughout the book, it will reference websites that will help you further.

Most of the subjects will have some relevance to you, or at least will start to make you think about them. That is the first step to a secure financial future. Start thinking about your financial future, start taking responsibility for your financial future and be knowledgeable enough to ask the right questions. If I can do that for you, I accomplished my goal with this book. Depending on your circumstances, maybe you ought to consult with a financial professional, as financial management is complex and a professional advisor can be of great value to you.

Taking responsibility is a big thing for me. Taking financial responsibility is the only route to financial security, as you will hear a few more times in this book. Always remember, you are the one that cares the most about your money.

Take your time reading all the chapters. At the end of each chapter, I ask you to create an action list. I have added some pages at the end of the book to take notes to create that action list that you can implement. If you have questions, go to my blog at www.FinancialSolutionsBox.com where I will delve into some of the questions that my readers have.

Thank you,

Patrick Peterhans - CFP®

Table of Contents

Chapter 1: My Story

I have always loved the financial markets and money. It shocked my parents when I was 12 years old that I wanted to close my savings account and open a brokerage account because it just made no sense to me to see so little return in a savings account.

Growing up in Switzerland during the late 70s and early 80s, investing in stocks was very expensive for someone who only had a few thousand dollars, since stock investing was the realm of the wealthy.

Nevertheless, I got my feet wet investing in some Swiss blue-chip companies, having to pay 5% or more in commission. I made some good moves, obviously I had some losers as well. However, the Swiss market was not that exciting, and I decided I had to diversify.

I found that some Southern European markets were really hot and decided to move some of my money into there. I had some big winners, but also as many big losers over the coming months and I learned a big lesson right there:

Understand what you are investing in, and if you don't, let the people who do know do the investing. Investing into a professionally managed fund can accomplish the same goal.

I have learned a lot from the crash in October 1987, the raging bull market of the 90s, and the following bear market during the early part of this decade, at which time I was managing money for clients as well.

Over the years I have also learned that being knowledgeable about other subjects beside just the investment part is equally important for a safe financial future.   The greatest enemy for most people in their financial success is their mind, and I will devote a whole chapter to that.

I used the experience that I gained with my clients in securing their safe financial future as well as my own to create this book. I hope I can convey this knowledge to you, my readers, as well. Besides my hands-on experience, I am a graduate of the Entrepreneur Program at the Business School at the University of Southern California in Los Angeles, a Certified Financial Planner and a Registered Investment Advisor.

I am married and have three children. We live on the beautiful Front Range of Colorado, just outside Boulder.   We enjoy the outdoors and everything that this part of the country has to offer all year round. I moved to the United States in 1987, and after living in Los Angeles for six years, I moved to Boulder.

Chapter 2: Risk Management

This is very important and an often neglected subject by many people.   This is also an area where people spend way too much money for something they don't need, but on the other hand decide to not spread the risk and expose their family as well as themselves to potential financial ruin.

There are three areas of risk management.

➢ The first area is where you pay someone to share the risk with you (Insurance).

➢ The second one is analyzing the risk; engage in due diligence for any given financial investment or business endeavor.

➢ The third area is the perception of risk.

Although this is not a very exciting subject for most people, not paying close attention to this could mean financial ruin faster than just about anything else.

Part A: Share the Risk with a Third Party

This is also called buying insurance. One of my guidelines on whether you need some insurance is the following: If you are not willing or able to write a check for a loss, you need some coverage.

Take personal responsibility and budget for it. The peace of mind will greatly enhance your life and put you on the right financial path.

The following are the different forms of coverage that you need to give some thought to:

Health

Having some kind of health insurance coverage is a must; at least a catastrophic plan if you are young and feel invincible. Many of us have coverage through work, and these plans are usually quite good. The laws are different in every state, and plans can only be sold in one state.

Many of you that are healthy should go with a higher deductible plan that lets you put money into a Health Savings Account. Higher deductibles scare many people because they are worried about that high expense sometime down the road. Think about it, when was the last time you had medical expenses in the four digits? I am sure for many of us it has been years, unless you've had a pregnancy lately.

For those of you working for a large company and have a very comprehensive plan, the cost for your employer is likely in excess of $8,000. This is part of the computation for the overall cost of employing you. What about going with a higher deductible plan that might cut the cost in half? Get an extra $4,000, pocket half of that and spend the other half on health items not covered. Encourage your employer to go that route.

I love Health Savings Accounts, but they also require that you take responsibility for your own actions. This means that minor health costs are costs of being alive, just like food, and for the big expenses we hedge. Health Savings Accounts also come with a gift from Uncle Sam, as any contribution up to a limit is deductible and any return on the money is tax-free. Obviously the money can only be used for health related expenses; otherwise the government will charge you a penalty.

Group coverage is in some cases the better choice than individual coverage (depends very much on the state). Starting your own business, even if it is just part-time, will open the door to different group health coverage.

You might find some good deals online, but this is actually one area where I always use my agent. His knowledge and access to different companies make this worthwhile.

To Summarize:

✓ You need at least basic, catastrophic health coverage.

✓ If you can choose a higher deductible, save money on premium and start funding a Health Savings Account.

✓ Start taking responsibility for your basic health cost yourself; this should not be a basic right covered by a third party, as food is not.

✓ If you can purchase your own, shop around to make sure you get the most coverage for your money.

✓ Work with a good agent who is knowledgeable about health insurance and is familiar with personal situations like yours.

Accident

If you have children, especially active ones between the ages of 6 and 18, you might want to consider an accident rider in addition to your health coverage. This is especially true if you have a high deductible. The accident rider is there to cover just about all of the deductible in case you have medical expenses due to an accident. You generally get family pricing on these, so the more children you have, the better the deal is. Your health insurance provider might provide that. I recommend that you check online for the best deal; it can be independent of the health insurance.

To Summarize:

✓ Consider accident insurance if you have children and if you have a high deductible health plan.

✓ It will cover most of the deductible if the medical cost is a direct result of an accident.

Disability

If you are under the age of 50, you are much more likely to be disabled for an extended amount of time than to actually die. Therefore, disability is as important as life insurance and even more important if you don't have children. (See life insurance discussed in the next chapter.)

Disability insurance pays you, after a waiting period, about 60% of your insured income. The premium depends on the work you do, and is much broader than Workers Comp because it covers also non-work related disabilities. Depending on the policy, they will pay after the waiting period if you can't perform your job up to the age of 65. Payments are generally income tax free.

Disability insurance is fairly expensive, but even if you have nobody depending on you, a must to have. You might have this through work, but just be aware that if you are in between jobs, you will not have any coverage, unlike with health where you can continue the coverage for up to 18 months through COBRA.

There are also short-term disability policies, and there are many options for the long-term policies.

If you can get the policy through a trade organization, you will save some money.

Social Security also has a disability program, but you have to be very disabled to qualify and the dollars will most likely not even come close to being enough.

I recommend that you talk to an experienced broker regarding all the options, or someone that is representing your trade organization.

To Summarize:

   ✓ Having disability coverage is very important to yours and your family's financial health.

   ✓ Think about what would happen to you and your family financially if you could not work for one or two years.

   ✓ Coverage through Social Security will not be enough in most circumstances.

Life

This is a policy that you hopefully will never have to use, actually you will not be here anymore if you do have to use it. However, your dependants will be most grateful and it might be one of the best investments you ever make.

Types of Life Insurance

There are two types of policies, term policies and permanent policies. I will talk here mainly about term policies, as you are looking to protect your dependants from a premature passing of the caregiver(s).

Term Life

If you don't have any dependants, there is no reason to have term life insurance unless you are planning to have dependants soon and are worried that you might not qualify anymore for medical reasons.

The term policy covers a certain period during which time your beneficiary would get the face amount of the policy if you pass away. After that period, there is no value in the policy.

Term policies come in different lengths from just one year to 30 years. The price is dependent on your age, your health and the length of term you choose. The term you need to choose depends on how long your dependant will depend on you. Therefore, if you have a newborn, a 20-year term might be appropriate, if your children are seven or eight years old, 15 years is probably enough.

You want to cover the money earners in the family to replace lost future income. If there is a stay-at-home mom or dad in your family, you want to insure the stay-at-home person as well, as that will give you some flexibility in a very difficult time. You will then either have to hire a nanny if your children are young, or you might decide to stay with the children and work part-time. You will not know how you react in that situation and you want to make sure all options are available to you.

Term life is quite cheap; hence it shows how unlikely it actually is that you need the policy.

You can shop for a policy online. Do a Google search, or a good place to start is www.selectquote.com.

You might have some coverage at work, but be aware that if you are in between jobs, you will not have any.

How much do you need? That truly depends on your personal circumstances.   Think about how much money with an annual return of let's say 8% you would need right now to pay your bills on a monthly basis, not even considering paying off a mortgage, college etc.

Term life insurance will also put at ease the designated guardians of your children, but more on that in the estate section.

Permanent Life Insurance

I just want to give you a few thoughts on permanent life insurance. They either come as Whole Life or Universal Life.   These are tax-deferred investments with death benefits.   They certainly have their place, such as additional tax-deferred money, for estate taxes among others. For most people they should not be a priority, as they cost seven to ten times more on a monthly basis for the same life insurance coverage because they are also a savings vehicle. You are much better off using your retirement accounts for your tax-deferred savings.

To Summarize:

- ✓ Purchase a term life policy to protect your dependants financially from a premature passing of a caregiver.

- ✓ Choose a term that is appropriate for your family's circumstances.

- ✓ Term life is inexpensive, so make sure you don't skimp on the amount of the coverage.

- ✓ Permanent life policies are a tax-deferred investment with death benefits. These are often too expensive to get the appropriate coverage.

Annuity

For all intents and purposes, this is a reverse life insurance. An annuity can provide you with a monthly income from the time of retirement until you die or a designated date.

The amount received depends on several factors. The first factor is the age you would like to start receiving payment. However, it also depends on the amount purchased, and the age when you purchase the annuity.

This can also be a diversification in your retirement plan, and provide you with peace of mind because it acts just like a pension.

As with all life insurance products, funds accumulate tax deferred, but most of the premium in the first year goes to commission, so this needs to be a long-term commitment.

This peace of mind is quite expensive in most cases. There have been some lower-cost annuities in the market place that could be worthwhile considering the right circumstances.

The bottom line is this: You are sharing or even delegating the risk of receiving some of your retirement income to a third party, and that has a cost.

To Summarize:

- ✓ An annuity is in a nutshell a reverse life insurance.

- ✓ It can give you peace of mind by giving you an income stream so that you don't have to worry about it.

- ✓ Buying such a security has its cost and needs to be looked at with other investment options in mind.

Long-Term Care

A good time to look at Long-Term Care insurance is when you are in your mid-50s because of its cost.

Whether or not you should get it is beyond the scope of this book, but issues to consider are the following:

- How is your financial health – could a nursing home stay ruin the financial security of a younger spouse during retirement?

- How healthy are/were your parents and grandparents when they were older? How long did they live?

- How healthy are you? Have you been sickly all your life?

House / Renters / Auto

If you own your own home, you will likely have home insurance since it is required by your mortgage company. Even if you don't have a mortgage, a home policy is very important.

If you own a condo, townhouse etc., make sure you have contents insurance. Usually the building is insured through your homeowners association.

If you rent your place, you want to have contents insurance as well; often that is called renters insurance.

Unless you have a very old car, you likely have comprehensive coverage on your vehicle beside the liability. Non-insured motorist might be a good thing as well.

It is important that you have sufficient liability coverage on all the above-mentioned policies, especially if you have assets. A good start is a 250/500 policy. The numbers refer to the amount of liability coverage in thousands.

I also recommend that you have a high deductible on both the car and house (at least $500), since these policies are not there to cover very small claims. Doing so will help you save money.

Having a higher deductible is another step toward taking responsibility for your own financial affairs and having money set aside (money saved by the lower premiums) for a rainy day. If you look at this over a longer period of time, in just about all cases the money saved is way higher than the occasional outlays.

Make sure you have these policies with the same company, as that will usually give you a discount.

To Summarize:

- ✓ Don't have a low deductible.

- ✓ Have sufficient liability coverage corresponding to your assets and that they are the same for your home and auto.

- ✓ Have all policies with the same company for discounts.

Umbrella / Excess Liability Insurance

This is another must-have policy that many people don't tell you about. This policy covers a potential liability in excess of your liability limits on your home and auto policies.

I am sure you are asking now, why do I need that? Well, we are living in a litigious society. Let me give you two examples:

❖ You are driving on a snowy, icy road slowly and responsibly. Suddenly you hit an ice patch and you slide onto the sidewalk and hit a dad with two very young children. The dad is disabled for the rest of his life, what kind of liability do you think you might have?

OR

❖ A true story: The wife of a friend of mine backed slowly out of a parking space and hit someone who was in her blind spot. Nothing really happened, the woman that was hit broke a few nails and had a bruise, nothing else. She was probably a little shaken, just like the wife of my friend. My friends were sued for $750,000 and the woman was actually awarded that money in the first instance by the judge after hearing the case. Fortunately, he had an umbrella policy, although only for $500,000, so he would have been out $250,000. They appealed and the next court reduced the award to $75,000, and his insurance company covered it, including attorney costs.

Make sure you have a policy with a one-million-dollar limit, possibly higher if your net worth is higher. A one-million-dollar policy should not cost more than a few hundred dollars per year.

To me, umbrella insurance is very similar if you look at it from a cost/benefit point of view to term life. It is unlikely you will ever need it, but if you do and you don't have it, it could financially ruin you and your loved ones.

You should get this policy with the same company that does your auto and house. If they don't have it, switch company.

To Summarize:

✓ Get an umbrella policy to protect yourself from the litigious society we are living in.

✓ This is one of the most overlooked policies, but when you need it, a very important one.

A Final Thought on Sharing the Risk with a Third Party

I know this is quite lengthy. I do not sell any of these policies in my practice, but I still feel it is important for everyone to know. Find a good broker, talk to friends and make sure you have the appropriate protection. In order to save money, you can always go with a high deductible. That is much better than skipping on one policy.

Action List for Chapter 2 - Part A: Share the Risk with a Third Party

Take some time and go through your insurance policies. Make sure they are appropriate for you, i.e. the deductible, the liability limits etc.

Go through each summary above and assess if you are exposing yourself to excess risk. Talk to a professional, but make sure you are not sold something inappropriate for your current situation.

Part B: Analyze the Risk of Any Financial Investment

Let me make a statement here:

> ➤ The biggest risk you are taking in any financial investment is not under-standing, not knowing what you are getting into. Buying anything just because you heard it was a good investment is foolhardy and the cause of why so many people lose money with their investments.

It is very important that you do your due diligence. If you can't or you don't have the time, have someone that you trust and has the expertise to do it.

If you don't want to research stocks and understand the company, have the stocks purchased in a packaged form by people who know what they are doing, i.e. mutual funds.

If you make investments outside the financial market, also referred to as alternative investment, become an expert in them or work with an expert.

Make sure you understand that you owe this to yourself and your hard-earned money.

Never participate in an investment that does not feel right or that you have concerns about and can't be explained to your satisfaction.

Risk can be very calculated and therefore reduced.

Don't believe the myth that a high return always has a higher risk than a low return on your investments, but you must understand the risk. (I will have more on this concept in the following chapters.)

Part C: Perception of Risk

We all have our own definition of what risk is. Here are some examples of why we perceive risk in a certain way but also why it is different for everyone:

- We all have conditioning from our childhood by our parents. Just because our mom or dad had a bad experience and consider something risky, it does not have to be that way. However, we look at it that way because that is what we heard as a child.

- Your own experience over the past years and decades. Maybe you lost money on something because you did not do your due diligence.

- The experience of a friend or acquaintance.

- It also goes the other way around. Some people make money fast, but not knowing or understanding what they are doing might make you lose the respect in the inherent risk of any investment. It is almost certain that they will lose some of the money again.

As I have mentioned, a high return does not necessarily equate to high risk. If you follow the mantra "high return equals high risk", you are shortchanging yourself in huge potential returns and its resulting financial freedom.

I believe sticking to the so-called "low-risk" investment is a very high-risk proposition and potentially unhealthy to your financial future. You will always belong to the "just getting by" crowd. Fear of losing or failure is our greatest enemy, and that is a risk you can't calculate.

Action List for Chapter 2 - Part B and C: Risk Management

Here is a little exercise before we continue to the next chapter:

Every reader should look at him/herself and be very honest about how they deal with risk. Write down why you think something is so risky or, also the reverse, not risky at all. Once you have done that, think about why you perceive it that way. Write that down. Also write down whether you could possibly be mistaken and what financial gain you potentially have foregone because of that perception. Think about and write down what you can do to change it by being more educated.

Chapter 3: Choosing the Right Investments in the Financial Markets

The United States has the largest financial markets in the world. The opportunities are huge, but all the options can make it quite confusing for many. I will try to lay out the basics.

The largest financial markets in the United States are the New York Stock Exchange (NYSE), NASDAQ, AMEX, and Chicago Board of Option Trading (CBOT). There are other ones as well. Every industrialized country has at least one, with some of the largest ones being in London, Frankfurt, Zurich, Hong Kong and Tokyo. There are some emerging ones in China (several in Southern and Southeastern Asia), Israel, Eastern Europe, as well as Latin America.

The investments in the financial markets should be the core of everyone's investment strategy. This is where you can invest and participate in every sector of our economy as well as the economies of the whole planet.

Terminology

Let me define some terminology first to make sure we are all on the same page.

- Stocks: Here you buy a small piece of ownership in a company. You might receive dividends, i.e. a small piece of the profit. The value is determined by the financial market and fluctuates.

- Bonds: Here you lend a company or the government money. They promise to pay you back at a certain date and until then pay you interest on the money at an agreed rate. The value of a bond does fluctuate depending on what the interest rates are doing. If you wait until the payback date, you will get back the full principal (unless the company goes bankrupt).

- Mutual Funds: Here you buy a basket of stocks and/or bonds of a certain sector of the economy. Doing that lets you own more than one stock or bond within the same investment category, like technology. This is generally less risky. Mutual funds are traded once a day.

- Exchange Traded Funds (ETF): These are a fairly new breed of investments. They became quite popular about 10 years ago. Without getting technical, they are very similar to Mutual Funds, but mimic all different kind of indices. They are traded like stocks. I often use them for specific sector investing.

- Options: These are more sophisticated investment vehicles and generally perceived to be more risky. In a nutshell, an option gives you the right to purchase or sell a stock at a certain price until a certain date. The right is the cost of the option. If you don't do anything by the date, the option becomes worthless, but potentially can be converted into the underlying stock. If you are interested in options, make sure you fully understand it and get some education. I will not delve further into them in this book.

- Securities: This is a term that often refers to the above-mentioned investment vehicles.

Now that we have the terminology down, let's talk about some concepts and all the different vehicles available in the financial markets.

Diversification

This is the Holy Grail in investing and can be summed up with one old saying: "Don't put all your eggs in one basket."

If you are not diversified, your exposure to risk increases dramatically.

A very well diversified portfolio increases your annual return over the years while reducing the fluctuation. What that means is that you will never have huge increases in value in one year like NASDAQ in 1999, but also you will not encounter the opposite, i.e. NASDAQ from 2000 to 2002.

Diversification also means that you don't just have money in the financial markets, but also look at other vehicles.

It does not matter how much money you have right now. If you have assets, look at the diversification of these assets and make adjustments accordingly. If you are just getting started, have a plan with the diversification concept in mind and then implement it accordingly over the years.

Emergency Fund / Cash

It is a must that you have several months' worth of cash at your disposal in an emergency fund. If you do have some unforeseen circumstances, this will help you get through them without liquidating assets. There are some good savings accounts online, such as www.Ingdirect.com that pays decent interest. They also have interest paying checking accounts.

Brokerage Account

In order to purchase or sell securities, you need to open a brokerage account. If you have an IRA, you will have to open a separate account for this retirement account. The brokerage account will allow you to do your investing. I recommend that you go with a discount broker, as the fees are much lower. I like TD Ameritrade, but do a Google search and see which one fits best for you. All the trading is done online.

Individual Stocks

For many of us, individual stocks are not the right vehicle. Most of us don't have the time to research the companies, and unless you have a large amount of money, you will not be able to achieve the desired diversification. Therefore, I recommend that you generally stay away from them unless you really know what you are doing. (See my comments next regarding "Play Money".)

There is one exception here for people who are looking for income from their capital. There are high yielding, dividend-paying stocks that can be a nice supplement to people who have regular income needs. They are in diverse industries such as financial, mortgage, oil and gas, shipping etc. You should be able to find some companies by doing research online.

Play Money

Some of you just can't stay away from trading stocks. What I recommend here is to have a separate brokerage account with a very small part of your investment capital. Don't include that as a part of your investment strategy, but it is money you are trying to hit a homerun with on stocks you think are going to take off. If you do have some homeruns, cash in and don't get greedy. Move some of that money into your longer-term capital or buy something with it because there is a good chance that you will lose it again.

Mutual Funds

There are hundreds of mutual fund families and thousands of mutual funds in the United States. Many have the same goals or objectives, although not all are equal quality. It is important that you narrow it down to a few mutual fund families.

All mutual funds have a focus. That means that they invest only in a certain part of the economy. Some examples are:

- Large-sized US companies

- Middle-sized US companies

- Small-sized US companies

- Industry specific, i.e. technology, energy

- Foreign companies or specific regions

- Bonds

- Hybrids, i.e. a combination of the above-mentioned

Almost all mutual fund companies have a fund that fits the goal of the before-mentioned types. Large mutual fund companies have several funds that fit each of the above categories.

Keeping diversification in mind, it is important that you know what the objective of each mutual fund is that you are interested in investing in. Buying three or four mutual funds from different companies that all invest in large US companies is not diversification; it is just adding costs to your portfolio.

How do I get the correct asset allocation?

Unfortunately, there is not a perfect answer to this because there are many factors that determine that. Here are a few:

- ➢ Your age

- ➢ Your health

- ➢ Your personal circumstances

One thing to keep in mind here is that you allocate these assets for the longer-term money. You don't invest money into mutual funds with the intention of taking it out again in a few months or even a year. If you think you may need that money in the next couple of years, this is not a good place for that money.

It is also important to note that markets fluctuate and that every allocation will no longer be good after a certain period of time. It is important that you reallocate some funds so that you can keep the desired allocation. This can be accomplished by selling appreciated assets, or often new money to be invested can take care of that.

There will be a strategy, lots of thought and reason behind your asset allocation. Don't change it on a whim. Make sure that there is a good reason behind it and that something actually changed from the time you made the initial allocation. That change could either be on a macro level, meaning it is on an economic level. Alternatively, it can be on a micro level, meaning you did more research and feel that this is more appropriate for you.

Let me give you a sample allocation for your mutual funds for a healthy 40-year-old with a steady income and accumulating assets. This then has to be tweaked if more income from investments is needed, or your health situation or your earned income is different. This is solely for illustration purposes, and you should do your own research to make it appropriate for you and the market conditions.

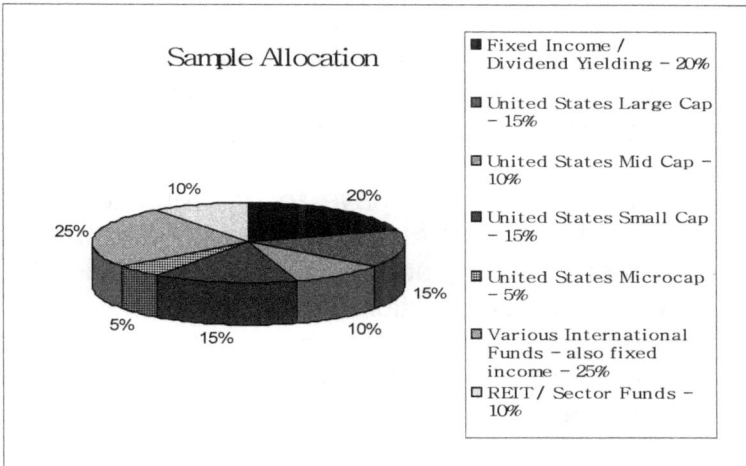

Sample Allocation

- Fixed Income / Dividend Yielding – 20%
- United States Large Cap – 15%
- United States Mid Cap – 10%
- United States Small Cap – 15%
- United States Microcap – 5%
- Various International Funds – also fixed income – 25%
- REIT / Sector Funds – 10%

How do I choose the right mutual fund company?

You want to look at mutual funds from two angles:

> What do they charge me to run the fund?

> What is their reputation, their track record?

Cost of a fund

Every mutual fund has a cost, since the administration and the running of the fund costs money. This cost usually ranges from about 0.2% to more than 2% per year of the money invested. You don't write a check for these fees, it is automatically subtracted from the value of the fund.

In addition, you have to differentiate between no-load and load funds. With a no-load fund, you will not have any additional costs; with a load fund there might be additional fees, sometimes of 5% or more, either upfront or on the back end. Loads come in all shapes and sizes, make sure you fully understand it.

I recommend that you only purchase no-load funds. If you are working with a commission-based financial advisor, then you likely will not have a choice. I don't recommend doing that either. (More on that in Chapter 15.)

Mutual funds are priced and traded once a day at the underlying closing price of the day.

Kinds of Mutual Funds

There are two distinct kinds of mutual funds:

- ➢ Actively Managed Funds

- ➢ Passively Managed Funds

Actively Managed Funds

A majority of mutual funds are actively managed. In these mutual funds you have a manager and his team who decide where to invest. These funds are the more expensive ones to cover all the overhead of running the fund.

There have been some very well managed funds in the past as there are some now. Unless you know someone at a mutual fund that knows a specific manager, it is very difficult to find a successful fund ahead of time. Once they are known, often it is too late to join the party.

Predicting the future is very difficult, and that's why actively managed funds often don't outperform the passively managed funds. Nevertheless, there have been some very successful mutual funds families, although once they get larger, outperforming the market becomes much more difficult.

Passively Managed Funds

They have a much smaller share of the market, but a growing one.   These funds are not actively managed.   The way they accomplish their goal is by mimicking stock indices.

These can be the well-known indices such as the Dow Jones Industrial or the S&P 500, but also indices that track industries such as technology, energy, health, financial etc.

Included in the fund are not only the stocks an asset manager perceives as having potential, but also every stock that fits into the category.   The theory behind this is that one cannot predict the future, and past performance is no indication of future performance.   Therefore, so goes the theory, one is better off to include it all.

People that subscribe to the notion that passively managed funds are the way to go believe that the markets are very efficient overall and predicting the future is very difficult.

What do I prefer for my clients and myself?

I use passively managed funds wherever I can. The reasons are the following:

- ✓ Passively managed funds outperform actively managed funds in the same category over a five-year period by a wide margin.

- ✓ Passively managed funds are cheaper.

- ✓ Most passively managed funds have many more stocks in them than the actively managed funds. That is what we are looking for in order to achieve maximum diversification.

- ✓ Outperforming the market on a consistent basis is very difficult.

I like funds from Vanguard, as they have a good selection and are low-cost. Vanguard also has some good low-cost annuities if that is something you are interested in. Vanguard's website is: www.vanguard.com.

For my clients, I use funds from Dimensional Funds Advisors (DFA). DFA only lets people buy their funds through approved financial advisors. These are phenomenal funds and you can learn more about them at www.dfaus.com.

Exchange Traded Funds

I have also used Exchange Traded Funds (ETF), which are in many ways like index funds with the difference that they are traded like stocks, i.e. all day. There are differences, but that is beyond the scope of this book. For all intents and purposes, they are similar.

Check out www.ishares.com, who was one of the pioneers in the late 90s introducing them to the United States market. Two of the most famous ETFs are the SPY (S&P 500) or the QQQQ (NASDAQ 100). Vanguard has some as well as well as www.powershares.com.

Bonds

Bonds are referred to as fixed income as well. I believe that it is important to have some fixed income as part of the portfolio, because it will both decrease the volatility as well as increase the overall rate of return over a longer period of time.

Bonds are generally best bought in mutual funds. There are corporate bonds, bonds from the United States government, bonds from state and municipalities (muni bonds) as well as foreign bonds.

The interest rate depends on the credit worthiness of the creditor as well as the market, and there are rating systems that rank them. Lower-quality bonds are also referred to as 'junk bonds', and they do pay a higher interest rate. If you consider junk bonds, make sure you purchase them in a mutual fund to spread the risk.

The value of a bond

If you intend to keep a bond until its maturity, the value of a bond will not change. Otherwise bonds can fluctuate in value considerably and I want to make sure you understand that.

A value of a bond will decrease if interest rates increase, and the opposite is true as well. The value of a bond will increase as the interest rates decrease.

The interest rate risk is the largest risk in the bond world, although a bond can also lose value as the creditworthiness of the company issuing the bond decreases.

As you can see, bonds have their risks as well, just like stocks, although it can be mitigated by keeping a bond until its maturity. This is not the case with stocks, as they don't have a specific lifespan.

The Magic of Compounding

We've all heard that the money should work for us. That is what compounding is all about. Here is an example:

You have $10,000 and you earn 9% on that money. After one year, you have $10,900. After two years, you have $11,881. Guess how much you have after 20 years? If you said $56,044, you were right. And you did not add one penny after the initial deposit.

So don't overlook that, time and rate of return are your best friends.

Action List for Chapter 3 - Choosing the Right Investments in the Financial Markets

Let's stop here now, and note what you need to do to get you on the right path. Go to the back of this book and write down action items for this part of your financial future.

These action items will differ depending on the amount of assets you can invest. If you have none, start thinking how you can start accumulating the assets. There will be more on this in later chapters.

Chapter 4: Looking at Alternative Investments

Alternative investments outside the financial markets have been booming over the past years. The beauty of them is that they provide additional diversification and there is not much correlation between them and the financial markets.

The rewards can be phenomenal. On the other hand they are not that accessible like mutual funds are. They also carry different risks, so getting your feet wet involves considerable due diligence either on your side or by someone you trust.

Many of them are small deals, kind of like family deals, where friends get together, pool their money and make an investment together under the umbrella of usually an LLC.

Here are some examples of what my clients and I have invested in over the past few months:

- 13 oil and gas wells in Oklahoma

- Real estate in Edmonton, Canada

- Mezzanine financing for an apartment building in Indiana

This could also involve buying a small business that requires a minimal amount of time commitment. Examples for that are:

- Vending Machines

- Laundromats

- Self-Service Car Washes

These are just a few examples. They all provide you with cash flow almost immediately. Be creative, be open and you will likely come across people that are also interested and you can form a joint venture, if you lack enough capital. I will get into more details how a small business can benefit you in some of the later chapters.

I know this sounds quite foreign to many of you, but that should not scare you away. Let your imagination run, read up on the trends in our economy and I am sure you will find opportunities.

Action List for Chapter 4 - Looking at Alternative Investments

Think about what you would feel comfortable doing on a part-time basis. Would you enjoy having some vending machines? What would you sell? What is hot right now?

Would you be open to alternative investments? If you think that is crazy, why?

Chapter 5: Know Your Net Worth

Definition

Everybody needs to know their net worth. The definition of net worth is the following:

Assets minus Liabilities equal Net Worth

Obviously you want your net worth to be positive. If your net worth is negative, I would say that now is a good time to start reversing it.

What am I Looking for in a Net Worth Statement?

I recommend that you have a line chart somewhere on a wall at home tracking it. On the horizontal line you want quarter/year, on the vertical line you have the $$ figure of your net worth. I recommend that you track that on a quarterly basis. Otherwise it just might drive you crazy. You also want to make sure the trend is upwards.

Why a Net Worth Statement?

Increasing your net worth is the only measure to see if you are on the right track to reach your financial goals. Just earning a lot of money will not do it. You can earn way into six figures and your net worth can still go down, if you spend it all. On the other hand, you could earn as little as $30,000 a year, and your net worth can go up if you are prudent about your spending.

I am sure you all have read the stories of old people dying with millions to their name, but they were janitors, school teachers, i.e. folks that don't earn a high income. Still they were able to amass large financial wealth by being prudent and watching their spending.

You have to figure out yourself what works for you, and we'll talk more about that in the budget chapter.

What Does a Net Worth Statement Look Like and What Should be in it?

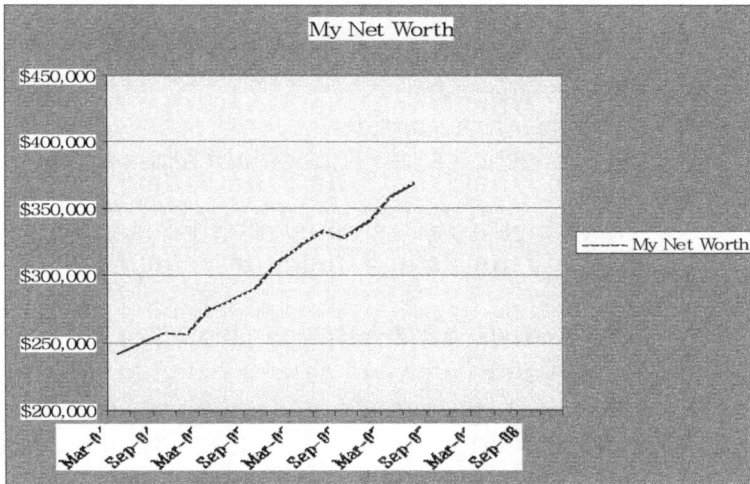

Have your Net Worth Statement on as big a piece of paper as you would like. Maybe you want to add a dotted line for the future goal of your net worth.

In Appendix 1 I include a sample Net Worth Statement.

Following are some examples of what fits into each category of the Net Worth Statement:

ASSETS:
➢ Cash
➢ Taxable Investments
➢ Tax-Deferred Investment
➢ Real Estate
➢ Other Investments
➢ Collectibles / Antiques (if of high value)

Don't include your car(s) and household items unless they maintain or increase in value.

The primary residence is a little bit of a question mark, as you will always need a place to stay and it is not a cash generating asset unless you have a reverse mortgage in your later years. Nevertheless, I would put it in while keeping that in mind.

LIABILITIES:
➢ Mortgage(s)
➢ Loans against Investments
➢ Consumer / Auto Loans

NET WORTH:
> ➤ Whatever is left over from deducting the liabilities from the assets

Action List for Chapter 5 - Know Your Net Worth

Now it is time to fill out your Net Worth Statement. As mentioned, there is a sample one in the back of this book, or you can get one from my website.

Enter all data from the most recent statements. If you don't have any statements on any assets, such as real estate, be realistic in the valuation. For residential real estate, you can go to www.zillow.com in order to get some idea of what the value is. Zillow is pretty good in areas where there are quite a few transactions and if your property is not too unique.

Start filling in the data with your current net worth every quarter and your line graph will start evolving.

Chapter 6: Planning for Financial Freedom and Retirement

A secure retirement and financial freedom is the main reason as well as motivator to do financial planning. In our society, we all focus on retirement as the time to have enough money amassed so that we don't have to worry anymore.

What is Financial Freedom?

The definition is very simple:

**Financial Freedom is when
your money works for you and
you don't work for money anymore.**

The amount of money you need for financial freedom is uniquely dependent on you. I will show you below that you don't necessarily need millions to have financial freedom.

In your planning, you never touch the principal while you are doing your calculations.

You also want to make sure you have more than one source for your income needs. That is actually true no matter if you are in the accumulating phase of life, financially free prior to retirement or in retirement.

The lifestyle / million-dollar question here is:

Are you content with a simpler life with the freedom of no money worries?

OR

Do you want your toys and luxuries at any price?

Either one is attainable, but let's look at the two options and what it takes to be financially free.

Example 1 – Simple Lifestyle:

Required Income: $50,000 per year
Annual Return: 9%

In order to be financially free, you would need $560,000 to earn the above income.

Example 2: Toys and Luxuries:

I will use a required income of $200,000, although some of you will say: Are you kidding, how could I ever live with that little money?

Required Income: $200,000 per year
Annual Return: 9%

In order to be financially free, you would need $2,200,000 to earn the above income.

I am sure you are thinking now, 9% annual return is pretty high. What about down years in the market?

I don't think you should invest all that money in the financial markets. What about one or two small businesses that give you passive income? Examples that come to mind are Laundromats, Self-Service Car washes, Vending Machines and your return will be much higher than 9%.

All these have some work involved, but are fairly passive and can be systemized considerably.

Action List for Chapter 6, - Part A: What will It Take for Me to Reach Financial Freedom?

What is important to me in achieving financial freedom?

Before going into more details of retirement / financial freedom planning, I want you to stop reading and think about the following issues. Write them down.

> ➤ How much money on a monthly basis do I truly need?

> ➤ What is more important to me: Financial Freedom or lots of money?

> ➤ Are you ready to take control of your financial life and well-being and be responsible for it?

> ➤ What will it take for me to take on this responsibility and to whom will I be accountable?

One issue to consider is the following: Once you have reached financial freedom at a low-income level, it does not mean you have to stay there. However, what it means is that you have the freedom to decide where you want to go, and money is not ruling you anymore, you rule your money and your life. Much more on that in Chapter 11: Your Attitude toward Money – Your Mindset

What does Retirement Mean for You?

Before going into the different vehicles available for retirement, I think every reader should think about what retirement is for him or her.

The following are some examples of what retirement meant for some of my clients:

- Work at leisure for fun and not money

- Travel

- Being close to grandchildren

- No worries about money

I am sure you can think of many more, likely it will be a combination of several desires.

Action List for Chapter 6, - Part B: What is Retirement for You?

Let's start defining retirement personally for you. Go to the back to the action lists and start jotting them down. Doing this is very important because if you have never defined it, how do you know what you are saving for? If you are in a relationship, have your spouse do the same.

Vehicles to Use to Save for Retirement

There are basically two vehicles you can use to save for retirement. One is the tax-deferred one, the other the taxable one.

The following vehicles fall under the tax-deferred category: 401(k), 403(b), all types of IRAs except for the ROTH, Keogh plans, deferred compensation and a few others.

These are great vehicles to save for retirement, but I would caution to not over-fund them unless you are planning to have a traditional retirement age of 60 years plus in mind. Maybe putting away money in a taxable vehicle is more beneficial to you and then using other tax laws to your advantage.

Let me give you a few advantages and disadvantages of the tax-deferred vehicles. I want to exclude the ROTH IRA from this list, as I will write separately on that one later.

Advantages of using tax-deferred savings vehicles

- ✓ Money grows tax deferred until you withdraw it.

- ✓ Income tax deduction for contribution.

- ✓ Employer matches / contributes to the plan (free money).

- ✓ Safety – money can't be touched for spur of the moment purchases.

- ✓ Most of the time professionally managed.

Disadvantages of using tax-deferred savings vehicles

- ✓ Forced withdrawals by a certain age and resulting tax bill.

- ✓ Withdrawals are all taxed as ordinary income, even if it is capital gain.

- ✓ Can't make a lifestyle change to live financially free without incurring huge costs.

- ✓ Very regulated by government – never know when rules change.

- ✓ Little self-control.

With the list above, I just want to provoke some thought in you. I certainly see the advantages in them, and there are also the self-directed IRAs that let you invest in many unorthodox vehicles.

Nevertheless, I have clients coming in who have $500,000 in their 401(k) and very little in their taxable brokerage account. Now they have to borrow against that money to start a small business that will give them passive income.

It is important that you have a nice mix. If you happen to have amassed a sufficient nest egg that would make you financially free by the age of 50, you would not be because you could not use that money without paying a penalty. (There are exceptions, but quite regulated by the IRS.)

ROTH IRA

The ROTH IRA is different from other retirement plans.

The biggest difference is that you don't have forced withdrawals by the age of 70½, and that the contribution is not tax deductible. However, on the other hand, any distribution after age 59½ is tax-free.

The maximum contribution increases in 2008 to $5,000 annually, $6,000 if you are over the age of 50. The maximum contribution will continue to increase in $500 increments linked to inflation.

There are limitations, but the ROTH is quite flexible and if you don't make too much money in the government's eye, you can contribute even if you have another plan at work. I like the ROTH a lot, and start one for your child if you can.

Retirement Calculations

I am not a big fan of retirement projections that tell you how many dollars you have to save every month at this rate of return and you will retire safe. I don't like graphs showing you how long your hard-earned money will last and when you will run out of it during retirement.

I do think it is a good idea to run some calculations to see if you are on the right path. I think all the projections have to be taken with a grain of salt, as these are just guidelines.

Nobody, no software can predict how things will work out let's say for the coming 20 years until you plan to retire, and then for the 30 or more years of retirement.

Having multiple passive income sources in place gives you the chance to maneuver the different circumstances that will be thrown at you. Planning for these sources will give you a good idea of what the income will be and whether it will be sufficient for your lifestyle.

Action List for Chapter 6, - Part C: Retirement Vehicles

Go through your retirement accounts. I recommend that you combine as many as legally possible. If you have old 401(k), 403(b) etc. from prior jobs, roll them over into a Rollover IRA. You can never contribute to a Rollover IRA, but it is a place to park all your prior work retirement accounts. Start taking control there as well. Make sure they are diversified. You can also combine traditional IRA's with Rollover IRA, but then you will not be able to move the money back to an employer sponsored plan.

Chapter 7: Have a Budget / Track your Expenses

Many people say to me, "Who wants to deal with the hassles of a budget?" My answer to that is: Everybody!

People tell me: "A budget... That is something that other people do, not me. Too complicated, don't have the time, I am not a numbers person."

Why a budget?

My firm belief is that not knowing where your money goes is the fastest route to financial ruin.

Some of my new clients have a good tracking system, most of them don't, but all will. Clients who start tracking their expenses always have surprises, even the ones that are financially responsible. I have a client who told me after tracking their expenses for a while: "I spent $300 on coffee every month!" Well, she decided to reallocate her resources a little.

The reason why a budget is so important is because you need to know where your money goes so you can make educated decisions on where to spend your money and how much extra you are actually able to save.

Doing and maintaining a budget does not have to be complicated. It should be as detailed as you would like it to be. I have one word of caution: Doing a detailed budget might discourage you from doing it over a longer period of time. You might be better off with a less detailed one that you can actually maintain.

How to set up a budget?

If you are tracking your expenses already, you can use those numbers as a benchmark. If you are not tracking your expenses, you need to track them first for a few months before setting up a budget. A budget is very personal, so it needs to be based on your circumstances.

Now you are telling me, "I don't want to track every little one-dollar purchase." I can understand that and my answer to that is to have a set dollar figure in cash per month that you categorize in the budget as 'Cash' and not track in detail.

As mentioned above, don't go too detailed, especially if the thought of having to do a budget gives you a headache and you are financially responsible, meaning you are cash flow positive every month.

Categories

Some of the basic categories that you should include are:

- ➢ Housing (including utilities, cable TV etc.)

- ➢ Entertainment (dining out, movies etc.)

- ➢ Groceries

- ➢ Auto – any transportation expense

- ➢ Cash

- ➢ Clothing – Beauty

- ➢ Children

- ➢ Education

- ➢ Medical

I do think that if you are financially in the red every month, you might need a few more categories.

In Appendix 2 I have included two sample budgets, a fairly detailed one and a basic one. These budgets will allow you to track your expenses on a monthly basis, as every column represents a month. This will also give you a nice monthly comparison on one sheet of paper to see where your money goes each month. It can also be downloaded from my website www.FinancialSolutionsBox.com.

What Systems Should I Use to Maintain My Budget?

I recommend that you either use one of the personal finance programs such as Quicken, Microsoft Money or a spreadsheet. Even though Quicken and Money are wonderful programs and can deliver lots of information, I feel for many people they are overkill. I prefer a simple spreadsheet, which is much easier to maintain.

As you can see from my sample budgets in Appendix 2, have a column for each month with the categories in the first column and the budget numbers in the second. Each time you are updating, just add the number into the corresponding cell. For the people who are not that familiar with Excel, enter the first number by typing the equal sign, then the number. (If the number was $24.50, you would type "=24.50".) The following expense ($15.50) is entered after the $24.50 (=24.50+15.50). Just keep on doing that and you have a running total.

How to Maintain the Budget?

I recommend that you use a debit card or credit card (if you pay it off every month) for all your expenses. Keep all the receipts, put them in a basket at home and enter them into your spreadsheet several times a week.

You want to make sure you enter these receipts regularly because you are not going to enter data if you have a backlog of several months. Doing it regularly has another big benefit: You always know where you stand and if you have been eating out a lot during the first half of the month, it might be time to cut back.

I don't recommend that you use cash except for the small items that are not tracked, since it is much harder to track cash.

You might find after a while of doing the budget, you want to know more information and add categories. Many people also change spending habits after a while, after all, knowledge is king and they set different priorities.

It is imperative that you enter **all** the data. It will be worthless if you enter only 90% of the data.

Summary:

- ✓ A budget is essential for a safe, financial future.

- ✓ A budget does not have to be complicated and very detailed.

- ✓ A simple budget is much more informative than a very detailed budget that has 90% of the data.

- ✓ Update the budget on a very regular, ongoing basis.

- ✓ Make sure you enter **ALL** the data.

- ✓ A budget will put you in the driver's seat of knowing where your hard-earned money is being spent.

Action List for Chapter 7 - Have a Budget

All I can say here: Start tracking your expenses. Check out appendix 2 for samples and download the files from my website if you have not done so yet.

Chapter 8: Uncle Sam - Income and Estate Taxes

Benjamin Franklin in a letter to Jean Baptiste Le Roy in 1789 wrote:

"But in this world nothing can be said to be certain, except death and taxes".

That certainly being true and taxes being a subject that has an effect on all of us, I want to make sure I touch on it. It could potentially have significant implications on your financial health by not taking advantage of all the rules and options. You don't have to give the government more than what is mandated by the tax laws.

Income Tax

Income tax laws are very convoluted and there are so many rules and regulations. The tax laws are also misused by many politicians to please their constituents. Here is some food for thought.

Statistical facts regarding income taxes

- ✓ Many families pay less in income taxes than in payroll taxes (Social Security and Medicare).

- ✓ Social Security and Medicare taxes are regressive and are especially punishing to the lower and middle-class earners.

- ✓ The top 50% of earners in this country pay 97.1% of all income taxes.

- ✓ The top 1% earners in this country pay 40% of all income taxes.

- ✓ Corporate income tax rates in the United States are among the highest in the industrialized world. This hurts global competitiveness and the taxes are essentially paid by the consumers.

- ✓ It has been proven all over the world that lowering tax rates to a certain point actually increases revenue for the government.

- ✓ There are hundreds of thousands of pages relating to taxes from the government that include the tax law, tax regulations as well as rulings and interpretations.

Tax Deductions

For many of you there are not many tax deductions that you can take advantage of unless you have your own small business.   Some of the more popular ones are:

> ➢ Mortgage Interest

> ➢ State and Local Taxes

> ➢ Charity

> ➢ Student Loan

> ➢ Health Savings Account

There are limitations on the mortgage interest, charity as well as student loan deduction depending on your income. The state and local tax deduction might be reduced by the Alternative Minimum Tax (AMT)

Tax Credits

The tax code also lets you take some tax credits for certain family situations or expenses you have. A tax credit is a dollar-for-dollar tax reduction on your return. A few examples are:

> ➢ Child Tax Credit

> ➢ Child and Dependent Care Credit

> ➢ Education Credit

> ➢ Retirement Savings Contribution Credit

> ➢ Foreign Tax Credit

There are limitations on these credits as well, depending on your income. The foreign tax credit has none and the child and dependent care credit has a bigger punch the lower your income, but both Mom and Dad need earned income in order to get it.

This is just a brief summary. Many people can do their own tax return with one of the commercially available software programs. I do recommend that you talk to a tax professional if you have any questions or doubts since the law is very complex. Spending some money with a professional could save you way more than the cost of hiring the professional. On the other hand, doing your own taxes might suffice just fine.

Estate Taxes

This is the tax bill you will not receive until after you pass. Potentially, this could be the largest tax bill in your tax-paying career. It is a tax you only pay once, as the government becomes a large beneficiary of your estate.

Here are a few facts:

- The estate tax is also referred to as the death tax or sometimes as inheritance tax.

- The beneficiary does not pay any taxes on the money received; the tax is paid by the estate.

- There is an exempt amount for which the estate does not pay any estate taxes. The exempt amount has been increasing over the past years, but the law is set to expire in 2011. The exempt amount per person will be as high as $3.5 million by 2009

- There is no estate tax between married couples.

- The gift tax is related to the estate tax.

- There will likely be new legislation over the coming years regarding the estate tax.

- In addition to the federal estate tax, there are also some state estate taxes.

If your estate is below the exempt amount, there is no reason to worry about it. Keep in mind; depending on how your life insurance policy is titled, the proceeds of the life insurance could potentially put you over the top.

Many states have their own unique laws in regard to estate taxes, and using a standard form that you can find online could possibly shortchange you considerably. I think for many people this is an area where you should seek professional advice from an estate lawyer.

How to reduce your Estate Taxes

There are many ways to reduce your estate taxes, but this would be way beyond the scope of this book to delve into in detail. I would like to show you three popular tools that everyone can take advantage of without using sophisticated planning tools. There are more complex and sophisticated ones available, but they should be used only after extensive consultation with your professional advisors.

Credit Shelter Trust

This is also called a 'By-Pass Trust'. The main reason to do this is to take advantage of both of the estate tax exemptions of a couple. Taxes on an estate that exceeds the exemption are as high as 45%.

Below please find a flow chart that shows the consequences of having a simple will versus a credit shelter trust. Here are the assumptions:

- Exemption from estate taxes: $2,500,000
- Total Estate: $4,500,000
- Tax Rate: 40%
- Husband dies first

The above assumption would then result in an estate that has $2,000,000 that is subject to estate taxes. With the 40% rate, this could potentially be $800,000 in estate taxes. Just doing a simple credit shelter trust can eliminate that liability to $0.00. I hope the following chart helps you to understand that.

Simple Will   **Tax-Efficient Will**

Simple Will	Tax-Efficient Will
Husband's estate $4,500,000	Husband's estate $4,500,000

	Wife's Estate $2,500,000
No Tax	Credit Shelter Trust $2,000,000
Wife's estate $4,500,000	No Tax
Tax of $800,000	No Tax
Children $3,700,000	Children $4,500,000
	Estate-Tax Savings $800,000

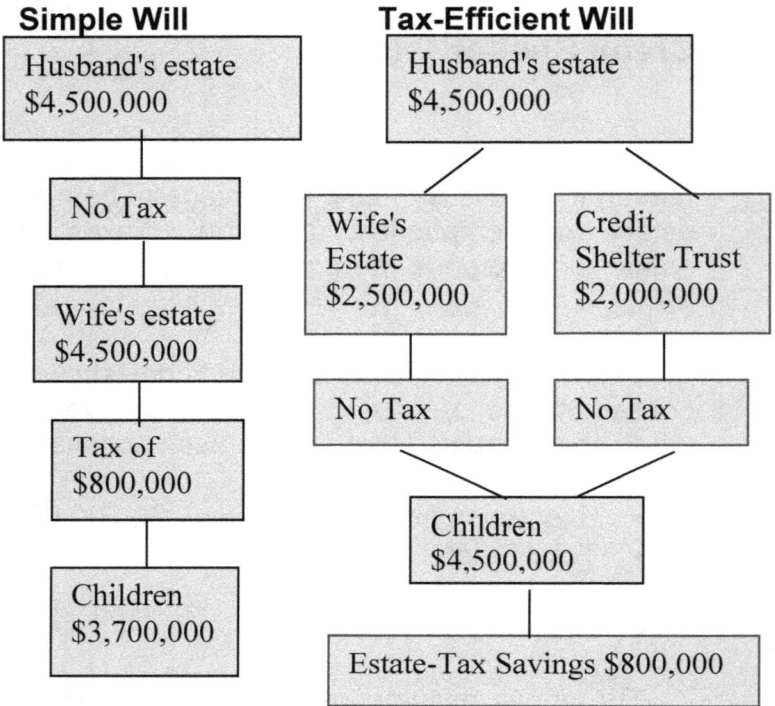

Assuming the trust documents are drafted correctly, the surviving partner can still benefit from the money in the trust, although the surviving partner will no longer have ownership rights. Once the second partner dies, the children will become the beneficiaries of the money.

Another advantage of this structure is that money is moved out of the estate before it can grow even further. This could cause additional estate tax liability once the second partner dies, which will be avoided if you use the trust.

Gifting

Currently you can give anyone $12,000 per year. That number is indexed for inflation. Married couples can each gift $12,000. This money is not subject to the gift tax exemption. Establishing a gifting program early on, while taking all the issues into consideration, can help reduce the estate and therefore reduce the estate tax liability. Keep in mind that the laws are complex and make sure you talk to someone to understand the ins and outs of this for everyone involved. This can also be used to reduce taxes on highly appreciated assets.

Charity

A fast way to reduce estate tax liability is to donate assets to charity. This can be done by donating to non-profit organizations. You can also start your own non-profit by filing with the IRS that you can use money for a good cause that the IRS approves of. Giving to others should always be a part of our lives, and by giving money to charity, your money will likely be used more efficiently than by the government.

Action List for Chapter 8 - Uncle Sam / Income and Estate Taxes

Your income taxes might be just fine if your financial life is not very complicated.

If your net worth is above the estate tax exemption, and you have not done anything to minimize the liability, I encourage you to talk to a professional.

Chapter 9: Protect Your Estate and Your Dependants

In the previous chapter I talked about estate taxes and many of you think: "This does not affect me." That is likely true, but one day you might be affected, and there are documents that you need nevertheless.

These estate documents are there to protect your dependants and your estate, as well as execute your last will according to the way you want it and not someone else. I will mention three different types of documents that you definitely need, and depending on your personal circumstances, they can be more or less sophisticated. If you are married, you need documents for each of you.

Testamentary Will, Living Trust, Trusts

The needed documents will depend a little on what state you live in. In some states, a simple Testamentary Will is sufficient, whereas in some other states a trust is an absolute necessity. Even though I recommend that you use an estate lawyer, make sure you are not oversold on documents that you really don't need. Make sure you understand the reason for a certain document, or talk to someone in the same state who is in a similar financial situation as you and see what they have.

Besides settling in this document who gets what asset after you pass, you will also decide on a guardian for your children. For my wife and I, that was a very difficult decision on whom we would want and who would be willing to bring up the children in case of our early passing. A guardian could be a family member or a friend. Make sure they have similar values to yours.

Assuming you will have term life insurance, there will be a significant amount of money coming your children's way. The best person to raise your children might not be the best person to handle a million dollars or more in sudden cash. Even though the money will be in a trust, having a person responsible for the money that has similar money values as you is a good option.

Medical Directive

You want to make sure you have written medical directives in case you are no longer able to make a decision regarding your medical circumstances. That includes if and how long you would like to be kept alive on a machine, whether or not you would like to donate organs and so on.

Power of Attorney

Make sure someone you trust, usually your spouse, has a power of attorney in case you are not capable of making decisions.

Have Your Assets in the Correct Name (Title)

It is important that all your assets are titled correctly. If you are married, it can be very advantageous to have some assets in the wife's name, and some in just the husband's name. With the right estate documents, this could help you save thousands of dollars in estate taxes. The example in the previous paragraph on Credit Shelter Trust illustrates this nicely, as that one will only work if money is titled correctly.

Even though I recommend using an attorney for all your estate documents, I want to make you aware of a good website on many legal issues, including estate planning. Check out www.nolo.com and click on the "Wills and Estate Planning" tab.

Beneficiaries of Retirement Accounts

We all have our retirement accounts. Some of you have many of them, since you have never consolidated them. Therefore, you have your IRA, your Rollover IRA at some bank from ten years ago, your 401(k) and so on. When you started the account, you designated a beneficiary, and maybe even a contingency one. Since that time, maybe your family situation has changed; therefore you want to make sure that for example your ex spouse is not the beneficiary of any account of yours. No matter what is in the will, the ex would get the money.

Action List for Chapter 9 - Protect your Estate and Your Dependants

Go to the back and check some of the issues I have listed there to make sure you have the appropriate documents.

Make sure all your retirement accounts have an appropriate beneficiary.

Chapter 10: Plan for Your Own Education and Your Children's Education

This chapter will be split up into two parts. First I will talk about the importance of continued education. The second part will be about your children's education.

Your Own Education

In order to continue to grow personally, it is important that you invest in your own continued education. This should be a part of your budget. If you stay stagnant, you will likely stay that way financially as well. Opening the mind will open you up to new opportunities which will certainly be financial as well.

Here are a few examples:

➢ Continued education at a college

➢ Seminars on personal development

> ➤ Seminars helping you with your financial well-being

> ➤ Learning a new skill

In order to be good at investing or any other subject, you need to become well educated in the subject, and that is true for everything in life.

Your Children's Education

Saving for our children's college is on every parent's mind. This should be a budget item just like retirement savings. Since for just about all of us there is only a limited amount of money available, you have to be careful that you don't sacrifice your retirement / financial freedom savings in favor of college savings. In my opinion, that is a major mistake. When planning for retirement, its commencement probably should not coincide with the time your children go to college.

There are multiple ways to save for college. I will mention four different options.

529 Plans

The 529 plans are state run plans, and the name refers to the IRS code. Here are some facts about these plans.

➢ One does not have to be a resident of the state where the plan is from to contribute.

➢ Each state has different plans with different investment options.

➢ The contributions to a resident's state plan are generally deductible on the state income taxes, but not in every state, and distributions are income tax free.

➢ The money can only be used for higher education expenses, including tuition, books and room & board.

➢ There are tax implications if the money is not used for its designated purpose as well as possibly a 10% penalty.

➢ The disadvantage is a possible reduction in eligibility of financial aid depending on your net worth.

➢ One of the parents should be the owner with the child as the beneficiary.

> ➤ The beneficiary can be changed once a year, so if one child does not use the money, the beneficiary can be transferred between siblings or even cousins.

> ➤ The money can also be kept in the 529 plan growing tax-free until the next generation is ready to go to college, or the parent can use it.

The 529 plan basically works like a 401(k) with different investment options. The investment options differ from plan to plan and some have age-based investment options, meaning the investment allocation changes automatically as the child gets closer to college.

Since you are limited on the use of that money, I don't recommend putting all the college savings into a 529 plan, just in case the child does not go to college or gets scholarships. As a guideline, I would not put more than the cost of a four-year public college into a 529 plan, the rest should be saved in other accounts.

529 plans can also be a nice estate-planning tool. Grandparents can open a 529 plan with the grandchild being the beneficiary. That could help them with their estate planning issues. Grandparents can contribute each up to a one-time investment of $60,000 into each 529 plan without incurring gift taxes. They can also use their $12,000 gift tax exemption to contribute every year.

In states that let you deduct 529 contributions, it might even make sense to contribute to a 529 plan the year the child attends college, just to take it back out a few weeks later to pay for college. That contribution will give you a state income tax deduction, but on the other hand that part of the tuition payment cannot be used when calculating federal college tax credits and deductions. Nevertheless, the cost is usually high enough that no deduction or credit uses up all the cost in a given year. There certainly should be some advance planning prior to the payment of tuition, books, as well as room and board.

One of the best websites to learn about college savings is www.savingforcollege.com.

Coverdale Education Savings Accounts (Education IRA)

These savings accounts have an annual contribution limit of $2,000. In contrast to the 529 plans, that money can also be used for secondary education. It also grows tax-free and has penalties when money is withdrawn for other than its intended purpose.

Regular Brokerage Account

Save money in a parent's name. There is no tax advantage, but also no disadvantage if money is withdrawn that is not for its intended purpose. The money in a parent's name counts for less when financial help / need is determined by the schools.

Alternative Investments

There are other vehicles that can help you with your college savings. If you purchase an asset during the early years of a child's life, the potential cash flow could cover much of the tuition payment.

An example for that is a condo. In order to make financial sense, make sure the cash flow generated by the condo is first of all helping you pay down the mortgage, and secondly creating positive cash flow.

At the time of college, you should have considerable equity that you will be able to use to pay for tuition, or possibly the cash flow will cover a nice part of it. Have the child manage the condo once he/she gets old enough. This could also be done with vending machines for example.

Advantages and Disadvantages of Different Savings Vehicles

Below is a chart of the advantages and disadvantages of the available college savings plans.

Type of Plan	Advantages	Disadvantages
529 Plan	Grows tax free, money out tax free, good estate planning tool, anybody can contribute	Possibly less financial aid, limited use of funds
Education IRA	Grows tax free, can also be used for secondary education	Only $2,000 per year, possibly less financial aid, income limitation who can contribute
Brokerage Account	No restriction how to spend money, less restrictive to get financial aid	No preferable tax treatment

Financial Aid

There are several sources that can help you with financial aid, and it might be worthwhile hiring a college consultant that has considerable experience. This is especially true if your child has a specific talent, athletic or otherwise, and the consultant could help your teenager getting scholarships at colleges that are looking for students with their ability. Merit-based scholarships are usually not based on the ability to pay. Obviously academics are equally important.

Money in the name of the child is weighted much more heavily against the qualification for financial aid than money in the parents' name. At the time of college, it might be a good idea to pay down the mortgage with money in a brokerage account, since home equity does not count toward the financial aid calculation. Money in retirement accounts generally does not count either.

In Colorado, the 529 plan provider also has financial aid services, and I am sure that is true in other states as well. Check out www.collegeinvest.org, the Colorado 529 distributor.

Action List for Chapter 10 - Plan for Your Own Education and Your Children's Education

Your Own Education

Go to the back of the book and start writing down what you would like to learn. Maybe you would like to take a knitting class, sign up for a certain seminar, go to a yoga retreat.

Your Children's Education

Do some estimation on your children's college costs. Maybe talk to parents and grandparents about it. Go to the back and make a list.

Chapter 11: Your Attitude toward Money - Your Mindset

A Look Back to Your Formative Years

Let's take a step back and look at some events that probably caused you to have a certain attitude toward money. Much of our attitude towards money was formed in our childhood, consciously and unconsciously. Let me list some possible events, and I am sure you can identify yourself with some of them.

> ➢ Your parents grew up in the 30s and 40s, and all you ever heard was that there was not enough.

> ➢ Your dad and/or mom told you over and over again: "We are not rich, we can't afford that."

> ➢ Your dad and/or mom told you over and over again: "Only rich people do that."

> ➢ Your dad and/or mom told you over and over again: "There is no way you can earn that much money honestly."

> ➢ Money was so tight when you grew up, either intentionally by the parents or for real, so that once you earned money, you had to catch up and did not remotely want to be like them and spend like crazy.

> ➢ At school or from your friends you heard: "Oh these rich people..."

I am sure you also had positive comments that formed your overall opinion of money. I am willing to bet that if you are struggling or not earning the money you would like, many of these negative comments are holding you back.

What Can You Do to Change the Money Mindset?

I believe that recognizing the issues holding you back as well as acknowledging them is half the solution.

What else can you do? Here are some ideas:

> Start reading books that talk about this.

> Attend seminars that deal with personal transformation.

> Look at the people you hang out with. Are these people in the same situation you are in? Maybe you need to look for new friends.

> How is the atmosphere in your workplace? Does that affirm your current mindset that you would like to change?

> Learn from people that are the way you would like to become, both financially and as a person. Copy them, they are your best role models, learn from them.

Your financial well-being is all in your hands. You only have yourself to blame, no one else, not your parents, the government, your boss or whoever else you can think of.

There is a good chance that you have to learn something new, change something in your professional life to get out of the situation you are in. I am not proposing a radical change, but be open to change and it will happen. You might have to temporally downsize to do that. It goes without saying that if you are not single, it will greatly help if you and your significant other can go through this together.

A change like that does not happen overnight or a few weeks. It happens gradually. Your mind will always take you back to your comfort zone, and you need to be alert to that in order to get to the next level.

I think no matter where you are in life, you can always improve on it. Unless you are financially free, don't just say I am fine, that does not apply to me. If you are self-made and financially free, you are likely the one that agrees with me the most.

Lottery Winners / Sudden Wealth

Most lottery winners are not mentally ready for their sudden wealth. That is usually detrimental to their newfound wealth, as most of them lose their financial wealth within a few years. Nobody can keep something, be it financial or otherwise, if they don't have the right attitude and mindset.

The brother-in-law of a friend of mine always just scraped by, never really having any money. He had many good ideas, but that was it. Nevertheless, with one of his ideas he made over $1,000,000, and that was in the late 1980s. Since he had the getting-by mentality, he was not ready for his sudden wealth and within three years he was financially where he started. He could not hold on to the money.

Earnings Potential and Mindset

One of my first clients when I only had my accounting practice told me, "I want to make $100,000 per year." Back then I thought that was pretty good because I was not making remotely that much. His income increased rather quickly to that figure. That was over ten years ago. He actually folded his business, took on a regular job and had kids. His income is still just around $100,000.

Why do you think that is?

When we met, he had that lofty goal of making $100,000. Then life caught up with him, and he never adjusted his goals but stayed at his magic number of $100,000.

Therefore, he stayed there, because that was his comfort zone. Make sure you recognize where yours is.

Staying in the comfort zone will not move you ahead. In order to advance, you need to step out and be a little uncomfortable.

Remember, it is you who calls the shots, no one else. I am sure your mind will tell you all the time: **"Oh not me, I can't, this is not possible, because of..."**

All I can say, these are just excuses from your mind. In order to get out of the comfort zone, you have to work on yourself and not stay on life's cruise control. So go for it for your own sake!

I have some links on my website www.FinancialSolutionsBox.com under Resources to books and seminars that I have taken that I thought were really good and helpful to me.

Action List for Chapter 11 - Your Attitude toward Money - Your Mindset

Think about what is holding you back and write everything down. Talk to your significant other about it; it will help a lot being somewhat on the same page. This is one of the action lists that is certainly a work in progress and can be merged with the first part of the following chapter.

Chapter 12: Couples / Families and Money

For many people this is a very difficult and emotional subject to talk about. Many of our attitudes and opinions were engrained at a young age as discussed in the previous chapter.

Let me touch first on the issue of couples and money, and then the issues of money for families with children.

Couples

Here is a sad fact:

Money is likely causing the most friction in relationships and is the most purposely ignored issue by couples.

On the other hand:

It is correct that money can't buy happiness, but it sure helps being on the same page and understanding your partner's money value.

Most of my clients are couples. Many of them have a very different opinion about some of the following financial issues:

- Spending habits

- How to deal with debt

- Perceived and real risk in their current or future investments

- Discretionary spending

- Budget

Who should deal with the ongoing monitoring of the family spending?

The resounding answer to that is the one that has a better feel for money and is more responsible with money. Those of you who are in a relationship most certainly know which one of you is the person to do it.

If you are the one that should delegate, don't let your ego get in your way, it is OK to delegate. Accept the fact and always keep in mind that you are doing this for the well-being of your family.

Action List for Chapter 12 - Couples

Before we move on to the second part of this chapter, let's go to the back to the Chapter 12 Action List - Couples.

Let's have both of you write down what you think are your strengths and weaknesses regarding finances as well as the ones of your partner. Then also write down what you think your partner could contribute to the financial well-being. Make sure this does not become a blaming game, but the start of a constructive conversation.

If it works well in your relationship, you can think about how to improve it.

Families / Children

My family and money

When I grew up, we never talked much about money in the family. Money was not scarce; it was always there.

On the other hand, I was never taught anything about money and how it works. Growing up I believed that there would always be money in the family, as my dad was a self-made millionaire. The year I finished college, my parents lost all their assets. After getting over the initial shook and disbelieve, I had very few tools to deal with my new situation such as needing a budget, making less in my first job than my allowance was in college. It also affected my mindset about money for years to come because I was not willing to do certain things for fear of losing.

During the following years, I learned, sometimes painfully, by trial and error as well as from friends the basics of money. I was still trading stocks, but otherwise my knowledge was dismal.

How is it in today's society?

I feel that we are failing our children miserably by not educating them about money. We probably teach them how to balance a checkbook. We tell them not to have any credit card debt and to live responsibly.

Who teaches them what the effects credit card debt can have on their financial well-being? Do schools teach them how much money in excess of the debt amount someone has to earn if you take interest and income taxes into account? I believe very few do.

I feel we have an obligation to teach our children this very important subject. As parents who were not educated about it, here is a motivator to start learning about money finances so that our children have a head start when they get out of college and don't have to make all the same mistakes in their 20s as we did.

Cash Flow Game

This is a game by Robert Kiyosaki. He is the author of the book *Rich Dad, Poor Dad*. The adult version is certainly good, and especially to see how one acts in certain situations and to also look at it from a big-picture point of view. It is a game and has its limitation to real life, and it is also quite expensive.

There is also a cash flow game for children, which we play with our kids. There are only very basic concepts, like paying for something with cash now versus charging it and paying a monthly payment. My kids are than ten years old, and they are enjoying it and get money concepts ingrained into them early on.

There are other ways of doing it as well.

What can you do to help your children?

As with anything else, don't treat your underage children like grownups when talking about money. I don't believe they need to know what the family owns, neither should they be made to believe that they might inherit money one day.

On the other hand, you want to teach them about money. Here are some ideas that could be very helpful at the appropriate age of the child.

Ten years old or less

- Instead of spending money right away, teach them to save it. Explain to them that if they save some money, over time they will be able to buy something bigger that they might want at that time. We did this when our oldest one was seven. The younger ones then learned from that when the oldest one was able to buy something down the road and they were not.

- Teach them to be price conscious. Give them a small allowance, maybe one dollar a week for a kindergartner. Therefore, if they want to buy something for five dollars, they will start thinking twice about it after a while.

After the age of ten years

You should introduce the following ideas slowly, as appropriate.

- Talk about a budget.

- Play money games with them.

- Have them see the impact of debt – maybe tell them true stories from your own life.

- Reward savings.

- You can go deeper for them to see what effect certain decisions bring on earnings potential.

I knew somebody who was able to give their teenage children a generous allowance. That allowance was treated like a salary. So the child had to pay taxes, give to charity, save as well as have a fixed percentage for fixed costs. The parents then put that money into a separate account for the time the child graduated from college.

It worked well for their kids and I thought it was interesting.

Whatever you do is better than nothing. Don't treat that lightly because many wealthy families send their children to camps for that. As we all know, learn from the ones that have done it right.

Action List for Chapter 12 - Families / Children

Write down what you as a family can do to better prepare your children. If you don't think you are capable of doing it yourself, talk to other parents and find a solution. This could be by families doing something together or to look at classes. This will be so valuable for your kids and a worthwhile investment.

Chapter 13:   Have a Set of Written Goals

This is another important part of your planning process for a financially free future.

Facts about Goals

Everybody who is financially successful has put goals down on paper that he or she wants to accomplish.

It is very difficult to achieve financial freedom without any goals because there is nothing that motivates you to keep going.

Why Have a Set of Written Goals?

- Reminder of why you are doing what you are doing

- Motivation

- All successful people have them

What Kind of Goals are you talking about?

To me, every goal has some financial implications. However, some of the goals have a direct financial relation like: "I would like to own five apartment buildings." Other goals are more lifestyle oriented, such as being able to travel or seeing the grandkids several times a year if you live far away.

What about the goal: "I don't want to have to worry about money anymore."

With appropriate planning, this goal is certainly attainable, especially if you adjust your life accordingly.

Short-Term Goals versus Long-Term Goals

I recommend that you split up your goals into two categories:

> ➢ Short-Term Goals

> ➢ Long-Term Goals

Short-Term Goals

These are the goals you would like to accomplish in the coming one to seven years.

Long-Term Goals

These are the goals that you would like to accomplish in seven years or later. This is something you are working for such as the time after the children graduate from college.

Make sure the goals are attainable, but on the other hand don't low ball. With each goal, write down when you would like to have it accomplished. Having this on paper will be a constant reminder. Identifying the goals and putting a realistic timetable next to it means that you are halfway there already.

Action List for Chapter 13 - Goals

Writing down goals often cannot be accomplished in just one sitting. Nevertheless, go to the back to the Action List section of Chapter 13. Start jotting down dreams that have been in your head for a long time but never put on paper as the start of your written goals.

Over time, feel free to consolidate or adjust the goals until you have clarity. Communicating with your spouse is an absolute must as hopefully your goals will be similar.

Then go for it and realize them!

Chapter 14: Have Your Own Small Business - Full Time or Part Time

Owning your own business is the fastest way to great wealth, as the majority of the very wealthy in this country have done just that.

A Small Business is Risky...

People are telling me, "Oh, it is so risky," or "I don't know what I could do." I think it is a lot more risky to have a job with one employer and one income source than to have a small consulting business with ten clients.

What happens if you look at your employer as your client? That's what the employer really is since they are paying you for your services. What happens if you lose that client? Well, you are out of work and income.

Now let's flip the coin. One of your top clients in your consulting business leaves you. Maybe you have lost 20% of your income, but you still have 80%.

Now you tell me what is riskier to your financial well-being?

Starting and Running a Full-Time Business

Not all of us want large companies, but if you have a good idea and are willing to work hard for a few years, you can create value in a few years that someone will be willing to pay you seven digits for.

What are some of the key features that all successful businesses have?

> ➢ Make sure you have a product / service that the market demands.

> ➢ Have systems that can be duplicated and understood by everyone.

> ➢ Set up the business so that it can run without you.

> ➢ Learn from the people who have succeeded in it already, have mentors.

> ➢ Don't think you are the expert in everything – seek advice.

> ➢ Surround yourself with people that are more knowledgeable about certain subjects than

you are. This can be virtual or by hiring them.

This whole subject of starting and running your own business will be a future book and can't be covered fully here. However, if you follow the above-mentioned points, you are way ahead of the crowd already.

Be an Entrepreneur and Not Self-Employed

One of the greatest pitfalls is that many people become employed by their own business and they work for their own business instead of the business working for them. Don't be self-employed, be an entrepreneur. Maybe you need to go into a partnership to combine talents.

Part-Time Business

Everybody should have some sideline business, even if you are employed as your main source of income.

Let's look at some of the advantages:

- ✓ You do what you truly love.

- ✓ It will help you with your taxes.

- ✓ It could become a nice passive income source.

- ✓ It will leverage risk in case you no longer have a job.

I cannot stress how important it is to have a small business, even if it is very part-time and on the sideline. You never know what will come of it. Many of my clients have that and this is actually one of my specialties in my financial planning practice.

Action List for Chapter 14 - Have Your Own Small Business - Full Time or Part Time

Go back to the appendix under Chapter 14: Have Your Own Small Business – Full Time or Part Time. Write down what you would like to do. If you don't know, start talking to friends, go to small business events and see what is out there.

If you own a small business already, think about what you could do to systemize it more. If you are one of them who are owned by their business, and you know who you are, ask yourself what can be changed to free up your life and potentially make it more valuable to sell and cash out down the road.

Chapter 15: Working with an Advisor and Where to Find Resources

On my website I have a whole page with resources that I think could be helpful to you, and some of them I have mentioned in the book already.

Let me elaborate what to expect working with a financial advisor, should you choose to do so.

Advisors Charge in Two Different Ways

There are two ways advisors charge their clients:

- Fee-based

- Commission-based

Fee-based Advisors

I am a fee-based advisor, so I am probably a little biased. We charge a fee, either hourly, as a retainer or for managing money, a percentage of the assets managed. We are never, ever paid a commission for what we are recommending to our clients.

We feel that this way is a lot more objective. We are not restricted to one specific fund family. We don't have to trade or sell you more mutual funds to make money.

Many of the fee-based only financial advisors are members of NAPFA, which is our trade organization. Go to www.napfa.com to find an advisor in your area, or contact me. I work with clients in different parts of the country. However, many people prefer someone local.

Approximately 25% of the financial advisors charge this way, with increasing tendency.

Commission-based Advisors

These advisors get paid through commission from the products they recommend. That is how the industry used to be, but it is slowly moving towards the fee-based model. Often funds sold by these advisors have a load.

There are also advisors that are somewhat hybrid, by generally doing work fee-based, but they also sell insurance.

Should I Use a CFP?

Financial Planning is not a regulated profession; so in theory, everyone can go out call themselves a financial planner.

Every financial planner who earned the CFP has done the following:

- Extensive education program

- At least three years of work experience in the field

- Signed an ethics agreement

- Continues to do continued education to keep the CFP mark

I think you want to make sure the financial planner you are working with has the credentials. You can go to http://cfpboard.org/search to find a CFP in your area or to verify if someone still has the certification.

If possible, talk to your friends to find a CFP.

Resources

On my website at www.FinancialSolutionsBox.com, I have links to multiple resources that I use and mention in this book.

Chapter 16: Final Thoughts

Congratulation, you read the whole book! I hope you got some useful information out of it. Hopefully, you have been able to implement some of the information by following through with the action items that you did while reading the book.

I hope you feel energized with the new knowledge. Maybe you also have some doubt that you can actually do this.

I can tell you one thing, you absolutely can. Get help where you think you need some. If you don't have the time to deal with your investments, hire a financial advisor. I work with people all over the country. If you prefer someone local, do that.

If you follow all the steps here in this book, you might not need a financial plan anymore, but a coach that follows up with you and some assistance with the money management.

Make sure you continue taking responsibility for your financial matters. It is too important not to.

To keep the momentum going, go to my website www.FinancialSolutionsBox.com and read up on the blog. Ask a question there.

Thank you for reading my book. I hope you received much value and I appreciate all feedback. Please write me a quick note to testimonials@FinancialSolutionsBox.com so I can see what worked for you and what did not. You can also go to the website and click on the testimonial bottom.

Lastly, if you have a friend who could benefit from my book as well, I sure would appreciate the referral by sending them to my website at www.FinancialSolutionsBox.com.

Thanks again and I look forward hearing from you soon.

Index

Appendix 1:   Net Worth Statement

On the following page, please find a sample Net Worth Statement that I have used for my clients.

A sample Net Worth Statement can be downloaded from my website www.FinancialSolutionsBox.com. You can find it under the Resource tab.

In the Net Worth Statement file that I provide for you, I have included worksheets for at least eight quarters so that you can start on it right away.

The last worksheet has a graph that tracks your Net Worth. Everything is formatted already, and you only need to enter the data. Additional worksheets can be added in later years and the graph can be extended.

Net Worth Statement

Date:_____

Liquid Assets / Securities			Liabilities		
Liquid Asset - taxable	$	20,000	Mortgage Residence	$	376,000
Investments - taxable	$	35,000	Other Mortgages	$	145,000
Investments - tax deferred	$	85,000	Loans against Investments	$	55,000
			Consumer / Auto Loans	$	5,000
Total Liquid Assets	$	140,000	**Total Liabilities**	$	581,000
Fixed Assets					
Residence	$	550,000			
Investment Real Estate	$	200,000			
Business Investments	$	125,000			
Other Investments	$	10,000			
Vehicles	$	15,000			
Total Fixed Assets	$	900,000	**Net Worth**	$	459,000
Total Assets	$	1,040,000	**Total Liabilities & Net Worth**	$	1,040,000

Appendix 2: Sample Budgets

As a part of the budget section, I provide you with two sample budget spreadsheets so that you can get going right away.

I am including two budgets; a basic one with just a few items and then a more detailed one. Because of space constraints, I only show you the first three months to get an idea. You can receive the complete document by downloading it from my website. I am also splitting up the detailed one onto two pages.

Use the one you feel more comfortable with. As I have mentioned earlier in the book, you are better off doing a simple budget that is accurate than a more detailed one that is missing data.

You can download these spreadsheets on my website at www.FinancialSolutionsBox.com.

Simple Budget:

Cash Flow versus Budget for 2008						
	Budget	Jan	Feb	Mar	Apr through Dec	Average per month
Income						
Money earned from Wages	$5,500	$5,500	$5,500	$5,500		$5,500
Investment Income	$500	$500	$500	$500		$500
Total	$6,000	$6,000	$6,000	$6,000	$0	$6,000
Expenses						
Fixed Expenses:						
Home (mortgage, util. etc)	$2,000	$1,950	$2,020	$1,990		$1,987
Groceries	$600	$620	$590	$580		$597
Car - Public Transportation	$500	$400	$520	$520		$480
Insurance	$400	$400	$400	$400		$400
Clothing - Beauty	$150	$70	$40	$280		$130
Savings	$350	$350	$350	$350		$350
Medical	$100	$0	$170	$20		$63
Taxes	$1,000	$1,000	$1,000	$1,000		$1,000
Discretionary Expenses:						
Travel - Classes	$250	$0	$350	$100		$150
Dining Out / Entertainment	$150	$60	$210	$170		$147
Cash - Play money	$250	$250	$250	$250		$250
Gifts - Donations	$200	$200	$200	$200		$200
Total	$5,950	$5,300	$6,100	$5,860	$0	$5,753
Net Cash Flow	$50	$700	($100)	$140	$0	$247

Detailed Budget:

Cash Flow versus Budget for 2008						
	Budget	Jan	Feb	Mar	Apr through Dec	Average per month
Income						
Money earned from Wages	$7,700	$7,700	$7,700	$7,700		$7,700
Investment Income	$2,500	$2,500	$2,500	$2,500		$2,500
Total	$10,200	$10,200	$10,200	$10,200	$0	$10,200
Expenses						
Long Terms Savings	10%					
Tax Deferred	$650	$650	$650	$650		$650
Taxable Savings	$370	$370	$370	$370		$370
Total	$1,020	$1,020	$1,020	$1,020	$0	$1,020
Savings for Future Spending	7%					
Home	$210	$210	$210	$210		$210
Large Purchases	$300	$300	$300	$300		$300
Travel	$200	$200	$200	$200		$200
Total	$710	$710	$710	$710	$0	$710
Play Money	8%					
Accessories	$50	$50	$50	$50		$50
Beauty	$90	$10	$152	$80		$81
Cash	$200	$200	$200	$200		$200
Coffee	$70	$80	$65	$75		$73
Dining	$180	$120	$250	$190		$187
Entertainment	$120	$20	$450	$20		$163
Sports	$100	$150	$50	$90		$97
Total	$810	$630	$1,217	$705	$0	$851
Continued on next page						

Detailed Budget continued:

Cash Flow versus Budget for 2008						
	Budget	Jan	Feb	Mar	Apr through Dec	Average per month
Continued						
Education Money	4%					
Children	$260	$260	$260	$260		$260
Own Education	$150	$150	$150	$150		$150
Total	$410	$410	$410	$410	$0	$410
Money for Necessities	67%					
Car	$300	$300	$300	$300		$300
Clothes	$100	$0	$250	$100		$117
Groceries	$750	$710	$690	$810		$737
Household	$350	$280	$210	$200		$230
Insurance	$400	$400	$400	$400		$400
Medical	$250	$0	$25	$300		$108
Mortgage	$2,200	$2,200	$2,200	$2,200		$2,200
Pets	$100	$40	$80	$60		$60
Taxes	$2,100	$2,100	$2,100	$2,100		$2,100
Utilities	$250	$325	$290	$240		$285
Total	$6,800	$6,355	$6,545	$6,710	$0	$6,537
Money for Gifting	4%					
Birthday / Gifts	$195	$195	$195	$195		$195
Donation	$210	$210	$210	$210		$210
Total	$405	$405	$405	$405	$0	$405
TOTAL EXPENSES	$10,155	$9,530	$10,307	$9,960	$0	$9,932
NET CASH FLOW	$45	$670	($107)	$240	$0	$268

Appendix 3: Action Lists

The following pages are your homework. I think this is actually the most important part of the book.

I always tell my clients that doing a financial plan and finding out where there are open items is important. However, if you don't follow up and implement, the best plan has not much value.

So I encourage you to do this, spend some time on it and act on the open items.

I will also have the Action List items available for download on a separate piece of paper on my website.

If you have questions doing this, please feel free to contact me through my blog on my website at www.FinancialSolutionsBox.com.

Action List for Chapter 2 - Part A: Share the Risk with a Third Party

Take some time and go through your insurance policies. Make sure they are appropriate for you, i.e. the deductible, the liability limits etc.

Go through each summary in Chapter 2 and assess if you are exposing yourself to excess risk. Talk to a professional, but make sure you are not sold something inappropriate for you current situation.

Action List for Chapter 2 - Part B and C: Risk Management

Every reader should look at him/herself and be very honest about how they deal with risk. Write down why you think something is so risky or, also the reverse, not risky at all. Once you have done that, think about why you perceive it that way. Write that down. Also write down whether you could possibly be mistaken and what financial gain you potentially have foregone because of that perception. Think about and write down what you can do to change it by being more educated.

Action List for Chapter 3 - Choosing the Right Investments in the Financial Markets

These action items will differ depending on the amount of assets you can invest. If you have none, start thinking how you can start accumulating the assets.

Analyze your investments to make sure you have a well-diversified portfolio and that you have cost efficient funds.

Action List for Chapter 4 - Looking at Alternative Investments

Think about what you would feel comfortable doing on a part-time basis. Would you enjoy having some vending machines? What would you sell? What is hot right now?

Would you be open to alternative investments? If you think that is crazy, why?

Action List for Chapter 5 - Know Your Net Worth

Now it is time to fill out your Net Worth Statement. As mentioned, there is a sample one in Appendix 1 or you can get one from my website.

Enter all data from the most recent statements. If you don't have any statements on any assets, such as real estate, be realistic in the valuation. For residential real estate, you can go to www.zillow.com in order to get some idea of what the value is. Zillow is pretty good in areas where there are quite a few transactions and if your property is not too unique.

Start filling in the data with your current net worth every quarter and your line graph will start evolving.

Action List for Chapter 6, - Part A: What will it Take for Me to Reach Financial Freedom?

What is important to me in achieving financial freedom?

Before going into more details of retirement / financial freedom planning, I want you to stop reading and think about the following issues. Write them down.

> ➢ How much money do I truly need?

> ➢ What is more important to me: Financial Freedom or lots of money?

> ➢ Are you ready to take control of your financial life and well-being and be responsible for it?

> ➢ What will it take for me to take on this responsibility and to whom will I be accountable?

Action List for Chapter 6, - Part B: What is Retirement for You?

Let's start defining retirement personally for you. Doing this is very important because if you have never defined it, how do you know what you are saving for? If you are in a relationship, have your spouse do the same.

Action List for Chapter 6, - Part C: Retirement Vehicles

Go through your retirement accounts. I recommend that you combine as many as legally possible. If you have old 401(k), 403(b) etc. from prior jobs, roll them over into a Rollover IRA. You can never contribute to a Rollover IRA, but it is a place to park all your prior work retirement accounts. Start taking control there as well. Make sure they are diversified.

Action List for Chapter 7 - Have a Budget

All I can say here: Start tracking your expenses.

Write down here what you have to change before you can start tracking your expenses.

Use the spreadsheets I provide on my website at www.FinancialSolutionsBox.com, your own or Quicken.

Action List for Chapter 8 - Uncle Sam – Income and Estate Taxes

Your income taxes might be just fine if your financial life is not very complicated. If you are unsure, talk to someone.

If your net worth is above the exemption, and you have not done anything to minimize the liability, I encourage you to talk to a professional.

Action List for Chapter 9 - Protect Your Estate and Your Dependants

Double-check with your documents to make sure you have the appropriate documents. If you are missing something, get it in order.

Make sure all your retirement accounts have an appropriate beneficiary.

Action List for Chapter 10 - Plan for Your Own Education and Your Children's Education

Your Own Education

The first step is to start writing down what you would like to learn, to get better at. Maybe you would like to take a knitting class, sign up for a seminar, go to a yoga retreat.

Your Children's Education

Do some estimation on your children's college costs. Maybe talk to parents and grandparents about it. Start making a list. There is much help in estimating college costs on various websites, including the ones I recommended.

Action List for Chapter 11 - Your Attitude toward Money – Your Mindset

Think about what is holding you back and write everything down. Talk to your significant other about it; it will help a lot being somewhat on the same page. This is one of the action lists that is certainly a work in progress and can be merged with the first part of chapter 12.

Action List for Chapter 12 - Couples

Let's have both of you write down what you think are your strengths and weaknesses regarding finances as well as the ones of your partner. Then also write down what you think your partner could contribute to the financial well-being. Make sure this does not become a blaming game, but the start of a constructive conversation.

If it works well in your relationship, you can think about how to improve it.

Action List for Chapter 12 - Families / Children

Write down what you as a family can do to better prepare your children. If you don't think you are capable of doing it yourself, talk to other parents and find a solution. This could be by families doing something together or to look at classes. This will be so valuable for your kids and a worthwhile investment.

Action List for Chapter 13 - Goals

Writing down goals often cannot be accomplished in just one sitting. Start jotting down dreams that have been in your head for a long time but never been put on paper as the start of your written goals.

Split up the goals between short-term and long-term goals.

Over time, feel free to consolidate or adjust the goals until you have clarity. Communicating with your spouse is an absolute must as hopefully your goals will be similar.

Then go for it and realize them!

Action List for Chapter 14 - Have Your Own Small Business - Full Time or Part Time

Write down what you would like to do. If you don't know, start talking to friends, go to small business events and see what is out there.

If you own a small business already, think about what you could do to systemize it more. If you are one who is owned by their business, and you sure know if you are one of them, ask yourself what can be changed to free up your life and potentially make the business more valuable to sell and cash out down the road.